CRADLING MONSOONS

POEMS
BY
SARAH MCKINSTRY-BROWN

BLUE LIGHT PRESS ◆ 1ST WORLD PUBLISHING

SAN FRANCISCO ◆ FAIRFIELD ◆ DELHI

CRADLING MONSOONS
WINNER OF THE 2010 BLUE LIGHT BOOK AWARD

Copyright ©2010 by Sarah McKinstry-Brown

All rights reserved. Printed in the United States of America. No part of this book may be used or reproduced in any manner whatsoever without written permission except in the case of brief quotations embodied in critical articles and reviews. For information contact:

1ST WORLD LIBRARY
106 South Court Street
Fairfield, Iowa 52556
www.1stworldpublishing.com

BLUE LIGHT PRESS
1563 45th Avenue
San Francisco, California, 94122

BOOK AND COVER DESIGN
Melanie Gendron
www.melaniegendron.com

COVER ART
Flaming Heart Study 2
by Jill Rizzo

FIRST EDITION

LCCN: 2010943511

ISBN: 9781421891965

CRADLING MONSOONS

ACKNOWLEDGEMENTS

Grateful acknowledgement to the editors of the publications in which the following poems have appeared, some in earlier versions:

Chicago Quarterly Review: "Letter to the Land of my Birth"

Cimarron Review: "Flowering"

Plainsongs: "Frida Finally Leaves Diego and Moves to Nebraska."

The Sow's Ear Poetry Review: "Whitman's Heaven" and "Deadline"

"In the Sixth Month," "Letter to Frida" and "Origami Girl" also appeared in the chapbook *When You Are Born,* editor Diane Frank, publisher Bluelight Press, 2005.

"Music Appreciation 101" also appeared in *Nebraska Presence: An Anthology of Poetry,* editors Greg Kosmicki and Mary K. Stillwell, publisher The Backwaters Press, 2007.

"After the Ultrasound, Week 12" also appeared in *A Bigger Boat,* editors Susan McAllister, Don McIver, Mikaela Renz, and Daniel S. Solis, publisher University of New Mexico Press, 2008.

"Comfort Food" also appeared in *Filling The Empty Room,* publisher Morpo Press, 2010.

I'd like to thank Art Homer, Teri Youmans Grimm, Jim Peterson, and William Trowbridge. Without your kindness and generosity of spirit, these poems simply would not be. My debt is tremendous. Here's hoping the poems in this collection might begin to somehow repay you all.

Thank you Carrie Helmberger, Liz Kay, Jennifer Lambert, Cara Lustgarten, and Molly O'Dell for your friendship and for helping me to shape my roughest of rough drafts into something workable, and, sometimes, beautiful.

I have to thank my small daughters, Sophia and Lucia, for making me a better person, despite myself. And Matt, thank you for asking for my hand and taking the plunge. We'll come up for air when we're old and gray.

My heartfelt appreciation goes to Elizabeth Jameyson, Liz Kay, and Tracy Baker for their editorial help during the final editing stages of this book.

TABLE OF CONTENTS

Music Appreciation 101..11

I.

Fallout, Albuquerque, NM, 1987..14
Origami Girl...15
Letter to the Land of My Birth..16
The Year of Conception..17
In the Sixth Month..18
3 AM, Latching On...19
When My Grandma Used to Visit..20
Come Back...21
The Barber's Heaven...22
What He Brings Me..23
How to Cook His Dinner...24
The Folgers Commercial...25
Not Too Late...26

II.

After the Ultrasound, Week 12..28
I Know the Neighbors Are Having More Sex Than We Are.............29
What the Farmer Knows..30
Picture Day...31
Sophia's Got Some Questions..32
After 13 Months of Searching, The Girl's Body is Found Five Miles
    from Our House...33
December in Omaha: Demeter Speaks to Me.................................34
Flowering..35
Letter to Frida..36
The Baby Wakes to Nurse Every Hour While Your Husband Sleeps..38
While Weaning the Baby...39
Don't Take Your Health for Granted...40
Fear of Flying...41
This City..42
Frida Finally Leaves Diego and Moves to Nebraska....................43
Midnight, Diego Remembers..44

Bad News..45
Wishes...46
Why I Write Down All Her Questions and Put Them in a Box
    Marked Sophia..47

III.

Comfort Food..50
Grandma's Heaven...51
My Mother's Heaven..52
The Farmer's Heaven..53
Pearls for Georgia..54
    Georgia Moves to Ghost Ranch, NM
    I
    II
    III..55
    IV
    V
    VI..56
    VII
    VIII
    IX..57
    X
    XI
    XII...58
    XIII
    XIV

    ***...59

After the Revolution, Waltzing Is Forbidden............................60
If Only We Spoke in Haiku...61
Poem for the Lost Poet...62
Whitman's Heaven..63
It's Almost Spring...64
What You (the Tall, Blond-Haired, Blue-Eyed, Smart, Talented
    Woman Who Keeps Hitting on My Husband) Don't Know.....66
The Other Side of the Story...68
Late August in Nebraska...70

About the Author..71

For my daughters

MUSIC APPRECIATION 101

Dad fell for Mom
because she looked like Joni Mitchell.
Nine shared rent checks and one pregnancy later,
my mom came home from the hospital to him going ga ga
over the new Steely Dan album. I don't blame him.

A self-made orphan, he cut down his family tree
to build a bridge from Kokomo to San Francisco that's still burning.

Before he taught me to ride a bike or throw
a left hook, he showed me how to hold a record
without touching its face, without leaving fingerprints,
scratches, evidence. My dad's proof
that ghosts exist. They come back for birthdays and Christmas.

From a distance, he watched me grow into shoes, corsages, suitcases,
and Greyhound buses. And there's a reason why a record reads
like a cross section of a fallen tree:
when my father pulls that album out of its cover,
a whole year of his life is right there,
circling like kids on bikes in cul-de-sacs,
waiting for him to start the turntable,
place the needle in the groove,
and call them back.

I

Fallout, Albuquerque, NM, 1987

We keep our hair in our eyes
and hiss at the girls in the hallway
who hang mirrors in their lockers, wear lipstick, look
like they actually give a shit.

Missiles wait
inside our mountains,
and we can't sleep
without the T.V. on. We see

our dads on weekends,
and our mothers, drunk on remorse,
take new boyfriends
and buy us ice cream
and cigarettes whenever we ask.

Everyone's parents playing house
with a full book of matches.
Ashes, ashes, we crouch behind the horizon,
accidents on the brink of
blossom.

ORIGAMI GIRL

They say you've got a thing for heroin.
They tell me things have changed,
that I wouldn't recognize you.

They say you're an origami girl,
guided by men's strange hands.
Yesterday, you were a fish,
today, you resemble a rose. Tomorrow
your mother will knock on the bathroom door

to find you blue
in the face.
With your legs askew,
your arms outstretched,
your clothes not on,

the medic will mistake you for a swan.

Though you're swimming in some ocean
I don't want to know,
I won't tell you to pull yourself together.
I remember our small chests rising and falling
as we chased each other around the yard,
and, in my mind, in girl-time,

I hold you
and unfold your lungs,
untie your tongue,
take the needle out of your arm,
pick your dreams up off the ground,
dust them off on my jeans,
and pin them back on your dress.

Letter to the Land of My Birth

Your sands promised
nothing but the parched Yucca that pricked
my fingers, drew
tears. When I broke open

your cactus to taste
its sacrament,
you taught me about longing.

With you, I learned to roll
my *rrrr's*, ignored
my mother's warning to *stay
out the arroyo*, answered
the calls of older boys
with, *chinga tu madre!* and hiked
the Sangre de Cristos.

A woman now, I make
my bed in my husband's
land, where blossoms
need no urging,
where acres, lush to bursting,
choke on their own green.

The Year of Conception

We drank milk from the carton, bought blueberries
in February, and kept a bare cupboard,
but for soy sauce and a sack of sugar.
We couldn't see past our hands,

used our mouths to find the way back
into each other's skin. We slept in,
stepped from one dream to
another, the days and nights fitting like train cars,
he and I, the only passengers.

Each morning, his fingers struck up a conversation
with my spine, while I held last night's dream up to the light,
an amethyst, between my finger and thumb,
so he could see its facets. This appetite

for each other, this lapse
of vision, is what called our daughter
to my womb. My blood, my breath, my body
slowly turning away from him
to tend to the stranger taking root.

In the Sixth Month

Your inner ear has fully formed.
You can hear now. I've heard
of mothers playing their unborn babies
Bach and Mozart because classical music
makes the brain's spatial connections
arc towards one another like the fingertips
of Adam and God in the Sistine.

I've played no such music for you, and maybe,
someday, when the boy you pine for
majors in architecture,
or when your brain goes cloudy
as you stare at your pop quiz in geometry,
you'll hold this against me.

Truth is, I can't bear headphones on my stomach,
won't force you to sit in the front row seat
of your mother, the auditorium,
while Pachelbel's *Canon* fires off the synapses
of your brain. For the same reason, I can't bring myself
to have your father recite French
or fractions into my belly.

No sonata or tongue or equation
could teach us what we're learning already:
that to be human is to be heavy,
to carry more than one heart inside you.

Without speaking, you and I are two fugues
coexisting. The armies of this world ought to blow up
their road maps and speeches and tanks,
put down their flags, and put
their ears to my womb—
take notes on how our pulses negotiate,
listen to how this belly stretches like an accordion, a peace accord
making room for the song of you.

3 AM, LATCHING ON

I.

Womb licked clean by delivering,
lost in my hospital bed
on the ninth floor of the North Tower.
In this fragile hour,
in this sudden city of milk
and coyotes, of stars watered down
by streetlights, I push the red call button
and ask the nurse for a sleeping pill.
This new daughter, swaddled
in silence, clutches my dreams
in her fist.

II.

Never mind the clamp,
the scissors the doctor handed
to her father. I'm the window
to her sky, she's the sky

to my window. I sit
in the soft holding cell of her hunger,
listen to her pulse
beat its wings.

When My Grandma Used to Visit

Repetition of empty liquor bottles on our counter,
crackle of bourbon poured over ice and Coke,

her steady hand and drowsy habits,
crocheting doilies and chain smoking in bed.

We fell asleep to the lullaby of thumb striking
lighter. With each drag she pulled death closer,
ignited the cherry's budding fury.

Smoke crept under my mother's door, interrupted
her dreams, made the bouquet she held smolder,
white roses crumbling to ash.

We buried grandma long ago,
but Mom passed this fear down to me:

a vision of flames encircling her bed.
It's an heirloom that can't be pawned off.

When I hear ice cubes detonate
under the amber weight of whisky,

my DNA unravels; these roots tremble, unfurl, scramble.

Come Back

For Reetika Vazirani (1962-2003)

Hang up that heavy black receiver.
You don't need to call those memories
and invite them to dinner again.

Throw away that decade-old bouquet of arguments
picked from your mother's garden.
You've kept them in water too long,

and your lungs have begun to crave the dirt.
Come to the kitchen. I'll open a jar of late October sunlight
preserved for days like this. You make the tea;

we don't have to speak. We can let our mouths
cosset their tongues, let our spoons, heavy with honey,
do the weeping. When were done, we'll cut

the hands off the clock, tie our hair
out of our faces, and clean the skeletons
out of your closet. We'll laugh about how

you used to dress those bones up in chiffon
and take them out to poetry readings, strangers
gawking as you stood behind podiums, slow

dancing with your misery. Come back, and we'll
stay home. We'll put down our pens and raise
our voices like empty beer bottles. Born

again into blue-jeans and sweatshirts, we'll grow
the hands of carpenters, become fluent in wood
and hammers; we'll break open those rib cages

and build a cradle lined with breath.
Together, we'll make a soft place for you to put down
the voices you carried night and day,
insistent and greedy as a newborn baby.

THE BARBER'S HEAVEN

The first customer of the morning wanders in,
a bald man with a beautiful woman on his arm.
Just a little off the sides, he instructs.
She takes a seat in the chair behind him.
Between snips, the barber glances at her reflection,

takes in each tendril falling
around her heart-shaped face
as she loses herself in *Better Homes
and Gardens*. He imagines her into his bed,
draped in a sheet, propped on one arm,

twining her hair around her fingers. He catches
her glance in the mirror, gives her a look that says,
*Come home with me. I'll cook you Angel Hair
with prosciutto, capers, and butter.*
Her eyes blink a slow *yes*, and he's across the table

from her, watching those fingers twirl the fork
as she lifts the noodles to lips moistened by butter,
stained with red wine. After dinner, she washes,
he dries. They linger at the sink,
and when he touches her hair, he feels the pull

of the fat bald moon hanging unashamed.
Music about this Marvelous Night rises
around them; fingers now gliding on piano keys;
bass notes plucked from black-eyed Susans;
a spring breeze strumming the trees.

He reaches around her waist and pulls her to him,
each note floating, falling,
littering their feet with tresses of evening.

WHAT HE BRINGS ME

Sometimes it's a rose, or an armful
of groceries. Tonight, he walks through the front door
with a good story, the key that promises to release me
from this small country, where the emperor is our baby,
and the mother tongue, *Mommy.*

Our daughter in bed, we set sail
on the couch. Voices hushed, bare feet
on the sands of her sleep, my husband,
with lungs full as a boy's pockets
after his first afternoon at the beach,

tells me about his day. Each word, a piece of blue glass
held up to the light. Every, *you should have seen it,*
an iridescent shell placed in my palm.

This is how the night breaks open:
he puts his lips against mine,
and I hear ocean.

How to Cook His Dinner

Olive oil warming in the pan,
break off cloves of garlic from the bulb,
crush each one with the flat head of your knife,
slip off the skin.

Slide the garlic into the pan,
watch it dance in hot oil.
Remember last night,
the stars trembling, in your ear
his breath.

Add broccoli florets. They must soften up
just enough to take on the garlic, salt, and oil.
Stir. Shift your weight from one hip
to the other.

When you think it's ready, pick out a piece
and taste it. Baptize his fire with your tongue.
Awaken your own hunger, what brought you
to this table.

THE FOLGERS COMMERCIAL

I'm folding laundry
when the music kicks in. I look up
at the television. Of course,
it's early in the morning. Of course,
the brother, away at college, made it home
just in time for his sister's birthday. Coffee brewing,

his younger sister takes the bow off the gift
her brother brought her, sticks it over his heart, says,
"You're my present this year."
I fight back tears,
though it's not even good coffee,
and these actors are working me
with ropes and pulleys.

My daughter toddles into the living room.
I blame her. That big head,
those even bigger eyes, surprised
to be breathing, delighted
with the air. She raises her arms
up, up, and of course,

the mom and dad come downstairs
to find their grown son and daughter
sharing a cup of coffee, *the best part*
of waking up. And now
I'm crying, weeping, really—
it's the red bow, the brother, the sister,
the yellow daisies on our counter
my husband brought me just because;
it's the boy they pulled from the river this morning,
our lilacs budding, last night's footage
of another woman keening in the rubble,
that music, so determined
to ruin me.

Not Too Late

My girlfriends are calling long-distance—Seattle,
San Francisco. They're thirty-two-pushing
thirty-three, almost-forty, worried their wombs
are uninhabitable, moons
scoured clean by *Cosmo Girl*
and nicotine. They need to know
what it's like. How will they know
if they're ready? Their clocks set
to detonate, my talk into the receiver
is all sweet. I decorate
my lair with pink roses and votives,
tell them over and over it's safe
to enter, that the love they'll feel is
indescribable. Maybe,
it's because I love them. Maybe, it's because
I hate them. I hang up without saying,
you'll give everything, and they'll take it.
I don't tell them, it's not too late
to turn back, that I labored until dawn,
and when the nurse put the baby in my arms,
the sun was just beginning
to set the city I knew on fire.

II

AFTER THE ULTRASOUND, WEEK 12

You should know your big sister is prone to stomping
small things. Not yet two
inches long, you're safe—
for now. Still, before your first breath,
I'd like to say I'm sorry for yelling,

for forgetting to pick you up
from school, for the coca-cola Slurpee
you can't have, for FM radio,
split atoms, American cheese,
and the ozone
hanging over you like a sieve.

Sorry for the 5, 6, and 10 o'clock news,
and for fattening you up with Disney.
I'm sorry for 13, Yellow #5, and mandatory
Pep Rallies. I'm sorry for your first French kiss,
for laugh tracks, Improvised
Explosive Devices, and Standardized
Aptitude Tests.

Sorry for footnotes, specifically, *Ulysses*,
for Depleted Uranium, Sunday nights,
and Eleanor Rigby playing on Musak
in Applebee's.

Someday, you'll come across
pictures of this ultrasound and of Saturn's rings.
I'd hoped more of this world
would be left
to your imagining.

I Know the Neighbors Are Having More Sex Than We Are

Look at the heavy zucchinis, tomatoes,
even a melon
unplucked
from their garden.
And yesterday, when I went
over to take them their paper, I saw,
through the window: plates stacked
in the kitchen, spaghetti sauce left to harden.

The Boston fern hanging
on their porch is limp
with drought,
and haven't you wondered
why you haven't seen the husband out
since he replaced their lawn with wildflowers
and buffalo grass?
Can you imagine?
No monthly yanking
of the mower's string.

All this time,
we've been working overtime,
saving up for our trip to New York,
and they've been acting
like they don't live in Omaha. I'm tempted
to take their Sunday paper
and pick those tomatoes.

WHAT THE FARMER KNOWS
For Julie

When sorrow sweeps in like a storm,
cumulous and furious,
you must drop to your knees

and ask the soil to break you
of your rage. Breathing
is about giving each seedling a name,

though it may not take.
Hope is backbreaking.
Even in dreams, feel the pull, the plow,

turning earth, soil so dark
it becomes night sky, and the seeds
in your hands, stars. Wish on

chard, tomatillo, basil, potatoes.
Never pray for rain. Walk through
the garden with dirt beneath the half-moons

of your fingernails, at your feet
each yellow squash blossom yawning open,
a newborn daughter,

the baby's mouth flowering
with hunger, what brought us
to the arms of our mothers.

PICTURE DAY

The night before, I tell Sophia
to remind her father to wash her hair
and comb it before bed. Her voice,
a yellow ribbon, she calls out,
Okay Mommy! Tomorrow

is picture day and this evening,
for the first time, she pauses
in front of the bathroom mirror, sweeps
her hair away from her forehead to get a better look.
Standing behind her, I move
to distract her. My hands on her shoulders,

I draw her away, and the moment
snaps shut. I want her to stay,
to keep moving through her days
as if she were air,
an invitation to sing.

I don't know how much time we have
before her hips blossom,
before her pupils sharpen
as she stands in front of the mirror,
taking herself in.

Come morning, I'll send her to school
with a purple barrette in her hair.
The earth spins, and I feel her pulling
away. Look how love breaks us both
in. She's learning to be still
for the camera, to smile and hold it.

SOPHIA'S GOT SOME QUESTIONS

The girl who began
as a single cell,
splitting and repeating,
a question my body
couldn't stop answering,
is now five
and a half, almost six,
and wants to know
if God made us with a hammer,
and if there are restaurants
up in heaven. Or toys.
Are there toys in heaven?
Is the dog going to die?
And if the dog does die,
will Jesus yell at the dog
for begging at the table? Is there yelling
In heaven? It's bedtime,
and she needs the unabridged version
of everything.
I do my best
to fit the cosmos
inside a goodnight kiss,
which, I guess, is fitting,
since the marriage of lips
and skin pretty much explains
the origin of her, girl
who spends her days spinning
in place, arguing with gravity
till we all
fall down.

After 13 Months of Searching, the Girl's Body Is Found Five Miles from Our House

Nights we sat down to dinner, interlaced
our fingers and recited The Lord's Prayer,
she was there, taking root, a seed
with his seed inside her.

Abandoned by the sun,
lost in the thick woods
of some man's fever,
we can't stop looking at our daughters.

And when the girl's mother appears
on the evening news, distraught,
but grateful for a body, I understand.

From the deep well of our wombs,
we draw our daughters up,
bring them to our breast,
quench a thirst they didn't know
they had, saddle them with hunger
so they might stay.

Let it not be his hands that claimed her. Let it be
the tender dirt, the earth slowly awakening
to her body as it softens in the sun,
preparing her,

each pearl of larvae working to ease
the burden, to release her
from the body that caught his gaze.

DECEMBER IN OMAHA: DEMETER SPEAKS

My grief strips your elm
of its crimson, whittles your days down to bone.
Streetlights awaken sooner, making mothers anxious
to call their children in for supper.

Pull the sky down around your shoulders.
Listen to the voices of those naked trees that keep my vigil,
their bare branches, like good sons and daughters,
bearing the weight of snow.

In these coming months, think, if you can,
of the frozen ground as a comfort.
This is the season when nothing else can be taken or given.
It's the only way to keep the world
from spinning.

FLOWERING

Mother sits across from me,
and the silence we share is tender,
falling off the bone.

In the cellar, her heart
sulks green, hard,
inaudible, her
aorta stumped
by my flowering.
I was a bulb
meant for quicksand, the vacuum
in the doctor's precise hand,
not the wetlands of her womb.

I held on, grew barbed
roots, and now I sit perennial,
a day lily flaunting
its soft tissue. I remind her
of her hunger,
how I fattened
her up, forced her to fast
from Saturday nights
at the piano bar,
where fingers once climbed
the trellis of her body,
slow and sweet.

Round and glazed, she sticks
her gaze on me, black
as black on the kettle of tea
fixed to her gas stove.
Blue flames shoot.
The water rises, gnashes
and screams.

LETTER TO FRIDA

Was it heated?
Body and Brain quarreling,
lovers locked in a room
in mid-June?

Brain says, *I love you*
body hears, *I loathe blue*
your hands give in

you paint the ocean red.

Frida,
the mouth is a wound
that refuses to heal.
I've taken to conversing
with hearses.
The dead don't ask
for things: they keep me company
while breath sits in my body's
fluorescent waiting room.

In your arms, the big men you loved
cried their small fears,
while your vertebrae, a set of teeth,
sank into you, deep.
All those days you argued with your husband,
who should have ripped down the moon
and used it to pumice
the corns on your feet.

Any real woman knows
flowers don't grow in rows,
you strange rose.
God, with gavel in hand,

had an eye on you. His pupil
fixed, an infinite bullet. Isn't it romantic, Frida, isn't it tragic?
How do you explain car crashes
on summer days when the light dances,
chrome tied up in flesh, shimmering?

When imagination stares at the walls
and I'm locked in this four-walled
body, I think of your helpless crutches;
the wheelchair dumbfounded beside your bed,
a foreigner that needs your body
to translate.

Frida, you bruised statue,
more than a set of eyebrows or wings,
you breathe red wombs
into my empty room.

P.S.
Por Favor, Señora,
write soon.

The Baby Wakes to Nurse Every Hour
While Your Husband Sleeps

You slip back into your old studio apartment,
into the arms of the lover who taught you
to read debris like love letters. You tore
into each other just so you could clean
the other's wounds. Once, he smashed
his guitar and laid the splintered brown
bouquet at your doorstep. He stood below your window
howling your name over and over, and then, *This
is what you did to me.* No more

overturned coffee tables and crooked blinds.
No more arguments rising like fumes
into the neighbor's upstairs apartment.
Remember how his pupils swallowed all the light
just before he punched the wall behind your head,
a black flower tucked behind your ear?

Daughter at your breast, husband curled
inside a dream. The vase on the bedside table
holds itself together, and you miss the wolf, wish
he'd blow this house down.

WHILE WEANING THE BABY

Your wife refuses to bloom in this room.
She is reneging,
digging up her ovaries and repotting them.
Your wife will sell those bulbs
at the farmers market to an unsuspecting blue-haired lady.
She must silence the bedroom,
unplugging the moon.

It is 1:53 in the morning, and your wife
is deleting her crown and giving you back
the ring. Your wife just heard that Blue
is the new Black and is reconsidering your eyes.
If you need her, she'll be outside,

watering her resentments in the garden.
Your wife doesn't love you anymore,
but she does love the geometry of her own indifference.
Your wife is checking the endorsements
on her driver's license. Her children sleep

sound while she interviews the abyss.
Your wife just took her heart
off the hook. The line is busy. For 95 cents,
you can get a call back.

It's 2:23, and your wife can be reborn
for only $19.95, plus shipping and tax.
It's 2:34, and your wife just knows she'll be born again,
if she can bring herself to turn the ignition key.
Your wife is attaching her voice
to this document. She'll send you her tears *par avion*.

the voice from the television scolds.
But, for a second, *don't take your Hell*

for granted, is what I hear, as if it's not obvious
that the angels are on their coffee break,
rolling the neighbor's prayers into cigarettes and lighting up
when he appears on our porch

to tell us its spread to her bladder, and there's nothing
to do besides hope she's comfortable while the cancer
unearths her. Death rings the doorbell, licks the envelope,
phones in, and the saints,

perched in their cumulous bleachers, boo
throwing cupfuls of cyclones at us.
My husband and I don't know what to do
except duck and cover

into the bedroom, offer our bodies up
to each other, exhaust what breath we have left.
We know we're kindling, and by the time the fire
grows large enough to illuminate the face that struck the match,

we'll be ash. So we rise
to meet each other and shed our clothes,
hands steadied by the lustrous feel of skin, the hand-spun lie
that the body won't break its promise.

FEAR OF FLYING

Gazing out my window, I sip
my Bloody Mary, soothed
by what lies below: fields of corn
and soybeans, laid out in right angles.
Every plan has a God.

Last week my brother called long distance
from his hospital bed to say
they found the infection
nesting in his spine. MRI,
Morphine, CDC, his voice

splintering. The doctors run tests.
I don't know anything
about mechanics or physics.
At thirty-five thousand feet,
it's hard to tell the difference

between God and engines,
fuel-lines and prayers.
My brother's sliding.
The sky stares back
with its singular blue eye.

This City

shows off its rage
while rats test peace
in a cellar lab.

The forest recedes,
gives way to murals
swarming with armies.

Bombs ripen. Vacant women
refinish their vanity, perform
for the looking glass.

Above, machines fly,
darken the pages
of Mother's dormant memory.

She reads the ground,
harvests her stare. Grief
greens and lengthens.

Drought eases
the sea into a bowl.
The stars crack, peel, splinter.
Soon they'll disappear

into textbook inscriptions.
Heaven's hinges complain.

No one is staying but the dogs.

Frida Finally Leaves Diego and Moves to Nebraska

I get up from the kitchen table
and walk into the blizzard
of my canvas.

By dawn, I've painted my little red brick house
with its single lit window. If you look closely, you can see
me, brush in hand, painting Diego

into my womb, the one place where he cannot possibly be
hungry. I listen to the second hand tap its pen against
the silence. The hourglass is empty.
My heart is a little girl banging on a grand piano
composed of black keys.

MIDNIGHT, DIEGO REMEMBERS

her hair falling,
her dress in a heap on the floor.

When Love was the wood
and the wound to be dressed, not the axe

licked clean and smiling.

BAD NEWS

Scorsese assured us
it would make its entrance
at 3 AM during a violent downpour.
We'd be snatched from our dreaming

by the ringing of a phone
some stagehand had placed
on our bedside table, just out of reach.

In May, after we'd put the baby down
for her afternoon nap, we took this as a promise.
On this day, surely

it was safe to answer. No one would call to say
that he was gone, that he'd done it
with a shotgun,
his passport in one back pocket,
driver's license in the other.

I hang up the phone and step outside, unprepared
for the sudden violence
of tulips
making their yellow announcements,
the grass so eager to green, beneath a sun, unmoved,
the breeze murmuring.

WISHES
For my husband

Once, I dreamt us childless in a park in Paris.
It was a spring afternoon, and you sat
cross-legged on the grass, my head cradled
in your lap, music piped in from the heavens. I closed
my eyes to better feel the sun against my face

and awoke to you standing over me,
arms extended: *Honey,*
wake up — time to take the baby.
This is how we stumble into each
morning, fumbling

with the names our own mothers gave us.
Before this daughter,
what did we clasp our hands
and ask for, what brought us to our knees? Love

struck a match, and she appeared, little flame
whose first cry lit up every corner of this city,
before burning it
to the ground. It's raining ash, and our wishes
are so small now

we could fit them on a single candle,
hold them in the palm of our hands.

WHY I WRITE DOWN ALL HER QUESTIONS
AND PUT THEM IN A BOX MARKED SOPHIA

I.

Sweetbitter unmanageable creature who steals in
our bed before the sun's fully risen,
I've not yet had my coffee and she asks
*If God made everything, did he make himself, too? How
did he do that?* I say, I don't know. *Ask
your daddy.*

II.

Did I know
that last night, in her dreams, she flew
without wings? I imagine her soaring above the trees, climbing
into the blue, and it occurs to me
we're raising her to disappear. I see
my face at the kitchen window
growing smaller and smaller until it's wiped clean
of its features.

III.

Before her coming,
I never noticed the dark.
Her asking is a match-tip
striking. She burns
bright, and it scares me, our shadows
thrown against the wall, everything
around us dancing wildly.

IV.

Now that she's here,
nothing sticks. When she's older,
I'll tell her that God made
us, and we made him in our likeness.

I'll tell her she's here
because, someday, her father and I
are going to vanish.
She's the best answer
we could come up with.

COMFORT FOOD

I come from a long line of women
who insist on cooking up a religion
that is more starch than cumin,
calling on a God who measures
blessings. Most Sunday mornings,
I can be found on my couch,
watching cooking shows on TV,
searching for a God who is more Julia Child
than Charlton Heston, imagining a heaven
that's one big small kitchen—a place
where all our souls will eventually rise
to sit around the table and break bread.

I can see my grandfather
passing the butter to his daughter,
while God putters around the kitchen
in Her billowing white apron,
measuring and mixing flour, sugar, baking powder.
She spills a little salt,
pausing to throw some over Her shoulder
to ward off the bad spirits.
And when a handful of it lands in the night sky,
She doesn't bother to sweep it up,
because She's not the cleaning type,
and She knows that all of us down here,
whose lives are messy,
more accident than recipe,
are hungry.

GRANDMA'S HEAVEN

No more VCR light blinking the same
sad midnight hour. No more falling
asleep to the lullaby of talk-radio hosts
promising rapture in the form of alien
abduction or plain old Armageddon.

No more arguing with ghosts
and browning the roast alone.
Or filling the kettle with just enough
water for one cup of tea. No more
hope or love or joy

or obligation to put the flag up
in time for the Fourth. No more shadows
with their abstract sorrows, or long Decembers
spent feeding the hungry black woodstove
of memory. No more doctors or agile smiles

or shiny tools licking arteries clean.
No more wincing stars, no more *now
where did I put that?* She's built herself a cabin
on the outskirts of the Milky Way, and she sits
on the porch in her rocking chair,

dressed in her red flannel nightgown and slippers,
a shotgun across her lap as she listens to the nearby creek,
a prayer, running steady and clear.

My Mother's Heaven

Morning breaks, a yolk in the cast iron pan.
Beneath lilac bedspreads in full bloom,
she lies sound asleep, sunlight
spreading across her face.

The nectar of small voices
wakes her from that other long
dream. Somehow, she's slept in,
and she rises and unfurls with ease,

her spine no longer forcing her to question
the ground. She enters her yellow kitchen
and finds that the children

are children again, and she, in her blue robe,
is famous for pouring juice and buttering toast.

Everything torn is mended.

The black lab they put to sleep
so long ago stretches
across the kitchen floor, easing
into a dream, his paws pulsing
as the coffee percolates,
the aroma meandering towards evening.

THE FARMER'S HEAVEN

He closes the gate and walks into that acreage of night,
rubbing his hands against the cold
as he kneels to hook the sun up to his blue tractor.
Climbing in the seat, he turns the ignition,
pushes it into gear, and begins the slow pull of dawn over horizon.

Below, the black-eyed Susans wake and tilt their faces towards him,

as the tiny flames of their petals catch and shake off last night's dew.
When he arrived, God told him,
over black coffee and Strawberry Rhubarb pie,
what his bones had been whispering all along;
City folks are more prone to weeping because they've forgotten how to pray

for rain. In the distance, our wide and wet-eyed dreams graze.
Slowly chewing, every so often they raise their heads to regard him.
He jumps down from his tractor, tears open his fat sack of clouds,
shakes out a storm. The rain begins its steady conversation with soil,
urging us to rise from our beds.

PEARLS FOR GEORGIA

Nobody sees a flower—really—it is so small it takes time—we haven't time—and to see takes time. . . —Georgia O'Keefe

GEORGIA MOVES TO GHOST RANCH, NM

Fresh from New York she
gleams and covets the women
with adobe skin.

I.
Here, blossoms rely on clouds
that may or may not gather.
I raise my brush.

                    II.
    White Jimson's   petals licked open by sun,
                her center,
            the color of butter.
                    Each
                    stamen,
                    still hidden,
                    waits
                    to be
                    strummed
                        by
                        breeze,
                        dew,
                        bees.
                    With
                    the
                    tip
                    of
                    my
                    brush,
                I draw them out of the darkness.

III.

This place is not so
lonely. At sunset these red cliffs
break their silence.

IV.

Who muses on what's
already been picked over
by crow, wind, sun, sand?

V.

Just before dawn, I wake
and step outside. Look at
that blue! How it deepens its hue

as if to hold out against the dawn.
Grace, each star flares,
perfecting its burning.

VI.

Stieglitz says he loves
photographing me because
he can't decide if

I am the flower,
or the vase
longing to be filled.

VII.

Harvest moon, burnished pearl,
hangs fat and low, a brooch
holding this night closed.

I reach out,
unclasp it,
let darkness slip from the mountain's
shoulders.

VIII.

When Stieglitz first saw
my paintings, he said,
if I had more lifetimes,
I'd give you at least two.

IX.

Chile ristra hangs
on the porch, a string of flames.
Hot kisses, dry mouth.

X.

The critics ask,
why bones floating against a backdrop
of blue sky? I have no answer.
They live inside words, and I,
in the spaces between.

XI.

It is easy to mistake
dirt for gold
if the sunlight hits it right.

XII.

Cow skull polished by
wind, sand, sun. My eyes pearling
with cataract.

XIII.

Tumbleweeds move
as if underwater. The sky
blue, parched and singing.

XIV.

I know Death is at
my back. While I breakfast,
she blows on the embers of my memory,

and flames rise without kindling.
Suddenly, I'm dancing
with Stieglitz, his eyes,

tiny bonfires, lighting the way.

* * *

Late fall. The wind has
taken everything. Still,
the bare cottonwood, with limbs raised,

praises the empty.

AFTER THE REVOLUTION, WALTZING IS FORBIDDEN

On the eve of our anniversary we always slip
Suan Zao Ren into the children's tea
so they'll sleep heavy. They're good children:
if they hear the hush of our bare feet waltzing
across the cold wood floor, they'll turn us in.

We pull the hard, brown suitcase
from under our bed and unlatch it.
He unfolds his suit jacket, and the crimson tie
slips out, a tongue cut from the mouth and set loose.
I reach in for my yellow dress, eager

to step into that whisper, to feel it
against skin. I turn away from him,
and hold my breath as he zips up the back
one tooth at a time. Turning to face the soft curve
of his grin, I take to tying his tie.

His hand settles on my waist
and we begin in silence,
chiffon moving against my ankles
like currents. With each turn we convince our limbs
that no one's watching. The children
are dreaming orchards in blossom,
and our feet are brushstrokes, wings
of magpies across that sky.

IF ONLY WE SPOKE IN HAIKU

Our engines fueled by
silence, we would carpet bomb
with cherry blossoms.

POEM FOR THE LOST POET

For C.A. and his son

We lean over the edge of the volcano, desperate
to see farther than our eyes will take us.
Our offering is meager—we light a word
and hold it over the abyss.

The sky above is an altar of silence.
The stars are stones, none left
unturned. Anchored by our lungs, we christen ourselves water,
cross time zones and borders, slip through

our lovers' fingers, leave them to make our beds
and lie in them. Their bodies, still fresh with memory,
curl towards our absence.
We must make our footprints in dirt,

paint, ink, stone. The breath can't hold everything we need
to say, and the heart, so rooted, does us no good.
Like an anxious mother, it repeats *stay stay stay.*
Somewhere there's a fire

waiting to be built, somewhere there's a tree
whose branches are ready to break and fall.
I've come here to gather and arrange them for warmth,
to light up the night, to try my hand

at God. See how the wood becomes both ash
and smoke in the same breath?
Can you see it rising towards the heavens? A language forgotten,
a beacon, a call, an answer, a psalm.

Whitman's Heaven

The silver timepiece he pulls
from his coat pocket has no face,
and his heart begins to stutter
when he sees the soldiers,
lounging on the grass, are whole again.

The breeze brushes the hair from their faces—
their eyes have not been dulled
by the grind of surgeons whetting
scalpels on their boot soles.

He rises from his wheelchair,
adjusts his boutonnière.
The restless hyacinths thrum
with bees. He joins the soldiers,
bums a cigarette, and lies beside them
on this ground that refuses coffins,
surrendering to every seed.

It's Almost Spring

which means I'm falling in love
with everyone. Yesterday,
it was the man in the produce aisle
holding his crying baby. The day before,

it was the twenty-something boy
at the coffee shop, perfecting
his disinterest while he took my order. Today,
I'm at the library, and it's the gentleman

sitting across from me, working out the crossword
on index cards he brought from home
so as not to ruin the paper for someone else.
Also, there are the children I can't see

but hear, thrumming, gathered
in a half-circle around the librarian
who is reading *Pokey the Puppy*
with great feeling.

Maybe I know what you're thinking:
Who cares or Where's
the metaphor or Didn't
Billy Collins write this poem

five years ago? But it's just
that the man's pencil pressed
against paper as he works out each letter,
makes such a great case

for silence. And the children,
loud as they are, are a fantastic argument
for rocking back and forth on your heels,
for forgetting to raise your hand,
for announcing your hunger or a full bladder.

Envious, I watch the gentleman work out the puzzle.
He finishes, rises, puts the index cards,
with all the right words, in his front shirt pocket,
the paper back in the rack where he found it,

the squares, empty, and he, set free, back out into the sun,
his body lighter for having found his way out of this poem
and into the breathless morning.

WHAT YOU (THE TALL, BLOND-HAIRED, BLUE-EYED, SMART, TALENTED WOMAN WHO KEEPS HITTING ON MY HUSBAND) DON'T KNOW

Though we're in a crowded room,
you say his name as if you were drawing a bath
for just the two of you,
as if you were lying
beneath him,
throat open, body reaching. You press

your hand into his, mistake me
for a ghost, a phantom, the woman
he's woken up with for the last
eight years.

What you don't know
is that he and I had the nerve
to get married outdoors,
in the evening,
in late October,

in Nebraska. That the morning
of our wedding, the sun rose
and unwrapped a blue sky.
That afterward, I got pregnant
too soon, told him in a grocery store parking lot,
bit my lip while he stared
at the steering wheel.

That when our first daughter came,
I clung to him and cried
for weeks,
our basement apartment overflowing
with emptiness.
You don't know how many nights
the baby screamed. How the moon looked on,
uninterested while we took turns

yelling at each other, wondering
aloud what the hell were we thinking,
wishing our hearts would just break
and not keep going. Like mules,
we took whatever we were given
and kept moving without asking for water.

You don't know how each sorrow
deepened the well, rekindled the thirst,
opened the doors for the second daughter
to make her entrance. On that morning,
he wept, gazed at me as if I were royalty,
took one look at the baby, said, *Honey
are you sure you didn't have sex with Winston Churchill?*

What you don't know
is that, if I so much as slip my hand
into his back pocket, if he so much as reaches
for my waist, we burst
into the Aurora Borealis.
You're stunning, but there are
thousands of people who drive
out of their way to find
our kind of beauty. So when you look deep

into his eyes, smile and talk out of the corner
of your mouth,

I won't put my arm around him
and drag him away. I won't kiss his cheek
lovingly. What you don't know
is that, when I walk away,
it's just my way
of staying.

The Other Side of the Story

after Dunn's "One Side of the Story"

My husband's started a to-do list titled, House
Projects. We make lists when there's so much
to be done that we forget what we need
to do. My husband likes lists because it's satisfying
to draw a line through something, call it finished.
We have two small daughters. We can't
draw lines through them. But we like to pretend there's some end
in sight, nights we slide into bed, turn towards each other,
and speak of all the things we'll do when they're older—
sleep in, take a trip somewhere far
but not too, Kansas City, maybe.
Just talking about filling our suitcases
with only what we need—a change
of clothes, a toothbrush—makes us feel lighter.
I just read a poem where the poet said,
I was thinking
so many people walk up to me
and tell me they're dead,
though they're just describing their afternoons,
and I think of us, in the dark, trying to find
ways to stay alive in our house. Maybe
we need a new list. There are days I want to sail
into a new area code in a baby-blue Chevy,
windows rolled down, the wind and Lucinda Williams
blowing through my hair. When that dream stales,
I cross the Atlantic, find myself lounging naked, smoking
on a balcony in Prague. Trouble is
I'm getting old enough to know
that the balcony and the Chevy
don't exist. And even if they did, it'd only be a matter of time
before I dreamed myself back

into this house, only a matter of time
before I started a new list titled A Way Out of Here or
A Way Back In, "In" and "Here" being relative
to where I am, which is beautiful
house, wonderful children, marvelous husband, and it's terrible,
getting what you want,
because that's when you know you'll always want
something different. And this afternoon,
I went to the library, read that poet's book, came
home, put the baby down for her nap,
and got on the treadmill. So am I dead, or
not? Whatever the answer, I'm pretty sure
there are days when you, whoever you are, are dead
too. And if we walked around alive all the time,
we wouldn't have our small resurrections.
Like my two girls. Like the cherry tomatoes I planted last summer.
The ones on my list. They actually grew.

Late August in Nebraska

Flanked by our small daughters,
we drift through buffalo grass and wildflowers in our yard.
You say our land shouldn't be so lush this late in the season,
that it ought to be dry to the bone.

Whatever the words used to describe what we've got,
they ought to be hard-earned.
I come from the desert, and when you asked for my hand
I felt rain at my fingertips, feared my own thirst,

shook with the memory of my mother's screen door
slamming, my father's footsteps fading into evening.
Call it record rainfall. Call it unseasonably cool weather.
We both know that love's not enough
to keep all this from turning brittle and breaking.

Our girls bend ceremoniously toward a black-eyed Susan,
bow their heads and inhale.

Winner of the Academy of American Poets Prize, Sarah McKinstry-Brown studied poetry at the University of New Mexico, the University of Sheffield, England, and the University of Nebraska. In 2004, she won the Blue Light Poetry Prize for her collection *When You Are Born* and has since been published everywhere from West Virginia's standardized tests to Omaha bus benches. Her poems have been featured on poetryspeaks.com alongside the works of Emily Dickinson and Lord Byron and she's been published in a number of poetry slam anthologies including *The Spoken Word Revolution Redux*, which featured Billy Collins, Ted Kooser, and Jeff Buckley. Most recently, her work has been published in *Nebraska Presence: An Anthology of Nebraska Writers, Plainsongs, The Sow's Ear, Chicago Quarterly Review,* and *The Cimarron Review.* Co-Editor of *The Untidy Season: An Anthology of Nebraska Women Poets,* Sarah received her MFA in Poetry at the University of Nebraska and lives in Omaha with her husband, the poet Matt Mason, and their two beautiful, feisty daughters. To learn more about Sarah, visit sarah.midverse.com.

Printed in the United States of America

CPSIA information can be obtained at www.ICGtesting.com
Printed in the USA
243427LV00002B/53/P

9 781421 891965